Care and Feeding of Tenants

Care and Feeding of Tenants

By Andy Kane

Illustrations by
Steve Soeffing

Paladin Press,
Boulder, Colorado

Also by Andy Kane

...And This Is the Bathroom! How to Really Sell Real Estate
Tenant's Revenge: How to Tame Your Landlord

Care & Feeding of Tenants
by Andy Kane

Copyright © 1981 by Andy Kane

ISBN 0-87364-240-6
Printed in the United States of America

Published by Paladin Press, a division of
Paladin Enterprises, Inc., P.O. Box 1307,
Boulder, Colorado 80306, USA.
(303) 443-7250

Direct inquiries and/or orders to the above address.

Contents

Preface

I actually became a landlord when I was nine years old. At that time my father passed away suddenly, leaving my mother to care for two small children and a medium-sized, two-bedroom Cape Cod home. Being a very traditional woman who desired to remain at home as a full-time mother, my mother hit on the idea of finishing the attic for our living quarters and renting the rest of the house. By converting the dining room into a third bedroom and renting the three bedrooms on the first floor to elderly women pensioners, she could obtain an adequate income.

The first tenant was an elderly lady whom we all loved and called Grandma. She had been born with only one ear and had deformed hands. She shuffled instead of walked, made weird noises when she mushed her food with false teeth, and smelled funny all the time.

The other two rooms were rapidly filled with similar creatures. As the big, strong man of the house at nine years old and seventy-one pounds, I was responsible for the maintenance of rocking chairs, doors, light switches, and other landlord duties.

Since most of the wretched old hags stayed with us until they croaked, I was also a witness to quite a few

deaths. I was always amazed at how long the other tenants mourned. Sometimes as long as three or four minutes before they began arguing and fighting over the deceased's coffee mug, radio, or rocker. Real nice people, these creatures called tenants!

I learned early that tenants are really not like you and me. I actually believe they have substandard mentalities. I don't like tenants and if I ever say something nice about one, please cut out my tongue. If you read anything nice about tenants in this book, write to me immediately so I can correct the misprint before the next edition.

My experience with elderly tenants lasted until I was in my twenties and about to be married. My mother had successfully run a rooming house for many years so she could bring up two wonderful boys, well, at least one wonderful boy. But now my beautiful bride and I were going out into the world to start our own household. I had set aside quite a sum for getting married—about $70, I think. Housing became a problem. If I rented an apartment I would become a tenant! The mere thought gagged me. I nearly vomited when I heard the word *tenant*. I didn't smell, eat funny, or shuffle when I walked. Me a tenant? Impossible!

I did not become a tenant. Instead I found a real estate broker whose specialty was apartment house sales and with his help and the help of two finance companies who each loaned me $1,200, I purchased a six-unit apartment house in a good area.

I got married on Labor Day and closed the title on the apartment house the next day. My honeymoon was two days long and we spent the rest of the time renovating our apartments.

Greedily I looked for ways to increase the take. I converted the coal-fired boiler to gas to make additional space in the basement. I put a studio apartment in the coal bin. I neglected to inform the coal company that I had converted to gas, however, and one fall evening the tenant came home, opened his door, and found thirty tons of coal! The experiences of being a landlord!

I did not become a full-time landlord until 1969. Before then I thought I could get rich some other way. I tried engineering, teaching, and designing, being an artist, a TV joke writer, and a pornographic cartoonist and driving race cars and trucks. I made enormous sums of money at all of these occupations, but one thing stuck in my mind. If I was out drinking or on vacation, raising hell or at an orgy, my income from all of these occupations stopped. Being a landlord pays me twenty-four hours a day, 7 days a week, 365 days a year, no matter what I am doing or where I am doing it.

I decided to get out of my full-time job, take my pension in one big check, and buy more apartment houses. Not as easy to do as to say. If I quit, I wouldn't get my pension in one big check and I couldn't collect unemployment insurance while setting up my real estate company. I had to be laid off. I needed the unemployment because by this time my beautiful bride had somehow quit her job and presented me with two screaming brats. They ate twice as much as I did and keeping rags on their backs cost a small fortune.

I carefully planned my dismissal. I grew a beard at that time when only beatniks and weirdos had beards. I did things to call attention to my department, to the embarrassment of my boss. I saw his hair go from brown to white in months. I showed a stag movie in the conference room and invited all the secretaries to attend telling them the movie was on a new company product. Within a short time, the company decided they could do without me. I made my exit, received my pension money, was eligible for twenty-six weeks of unemployment insurance, and a *year's* pay the company gave me to get rid of me! I immediately became a full-time landlord and I haven't regretted it yet.

In purchasing an apartment I met a wise, old owl who had been a landlord for thirty years and had vast holdings of lower and middle class apartment houses. I learned many new techniques from him about what to do and what not to do. I learned from him *not* to be good to tenants. He was good to his tenants. He would visit them in hospitals and bring them gifts. They still destroyed his property and moved without notice. I discovered being good to tenants is a waste of time!

I worked as a broker selling apartment houses until about 1975, when I started Andy Kane Realty Corporation and specialized in investment property sales. My

salesmen and brokers have come from all walks of life—
from Ph.D.s to high school dropouts, sexy chicks to
guys fresh out of the nut house. Nearly all have become
successful landlords, without previous experience.

At the request of many clients, I decided to compile
some of the techniques used in handling tenants into a
book. The name *Care and Feeding of Tenants* flashed
into my mind like a divine inspiration while I was visit-
ing the zoo with my two brats and noticed the similarity
between the baboon cages and some of my tenants'
apartments. The housekeeping was identical! As I stood
there watching the baboon and apes picking lice off
each other and eating them, I saw a great resemblance to
some of my tenants.

Read every word of this book, follow the principles
and methods outlined within. You will be a richer and
better landlord when you finish. Remember this one important word of advice: it's you against the tenant. Get
them before they get you. That's the American way.
God bless America!

1. The Landlord

As the word indicates, a *landlord* is lord over the land, owner of a vast estate, one who is due great respect. The word dates back to medieval times. It is also a word that in this day and age draws little respect. If you were to ask 100 people to draw a sketch of a landlord, 97 of

them would provide you with a picture of a sinister-looking man with a handlebar moustache, dark eyebrows, black top hat and tails, and a sneer on his face—the image of someone who had just tied a fair maiden to a railroad track.

More people in our country are housed in property owned and managed by small landlords like you and me than in any other type of housing. Landlords provide shelter for millions. Every city should have a statue erected to honor the landlords of our great country. Landlords, in my opinion, provide a greater service than the clergy. Yet clergymen get respect, discounts on air travel, tax exemptions, donations, and preferential treatment. Landlords get abuse. If you don't believe a landlord is more important than your parish priest, try standing out in the rain and wind with a Bible over your head. Shelter is mankind's basic need and landlords provide for that need.

I have never seen anyone receive more negative publicity than a landlord. Rapists, muggers, and mass murderers receive far fewer column inches in our press annually than landlords do. Television cameras roll at one call from a tenant who has just seen a rat in her baby's bedroom. The landlord is accused of being a slumlord, filling his pockets with rent, and neglecting his property.

Little attention is paid to the cause of the rat being on the property. The cause is probably that the tenants leave garbage in the halls or food lying around. I am certain that a landlord does nothing to cause a rat problem—he does not bring in garbage for the rats to eat—yet the media will definitely blame the landlord.

Why is that? Consider this simple fact. All tenants hate the landlord. *All* tenants hate the landlord. Deep down inside, no matter what they say, all tenants hate the landlord. I've learned to live with that fact and, personally, I hate all of my tenants. Keep that in mind in all your dealings and stay alert, just as you would if you were renting to poisonous snakes. Never forget that they hate you.

Consider what happens when a newspaper or TV station receives a call about the lack of heat in an apartment, rats or other tenant complaints. First, a reporter is assigned. This is not a presidential assassination, moon landing, or the Olympics. It's a tenant complaint. A cub reporter is assigned. He is a novice, $97-per-week journalist hoping to be another Walter Cronkite. No experience, just out of journalism school, wet behind the ears. Get the picture? Oh, one thing I left out. Is he a homeowner? No, not on $97 per week! He is a tenant himself. One of his kind is being abused by that villain, the landlord. He is going to look at this problem one way, through the eyes of a tenant. You are going to get both barrels.

The cameras will roll in your building, and since the TV crew would look ridiculous if they devoted their time to just the original complaint, a rat, they will look for other items to focus on, like the hole in the living room wall (the tenant's old man's fist went through the wall because she ducked when he came home drunk), like the defective light fixture (the tenant's brat swung on it), like the broken window pane (usually the glass can be found outside, indicating it was broken from the inside), and other signs of obvious "landlord" neglect (actually tenant property abuse).

Do we have enough now for the 6 P.M. news? Not quite. How does this landlord live, the landlord who neglects his property? The TV crew rolls up to 17 Palace Place to your palatial, seven-room Cape Cod home on a spacious quarter-acre lot with a mortgage nearly as big as the house. Amazing. No broken plaster, no broken windows, no rats. You villain! Does anyone consider the fact that you respect your property, your brats don't swing on the chandeliers, and you don't throw garbage around? Certainly not. The reporter (a tenant who hates landlords) will interview you regarding your slum. The reporter will ask all sorts of derogatory questions regarding your efforts to keep this property up to snuff. Anything favorable to your cause that you can inject into the interview will be edited out. The landlord remains a villain. This is the American way. God bless America!

Slumlords

Let me mention slumlords. I believe that our society could not do without slumlords. They manage the most difficult properties with the worst tenants and take a great risk of being killed or maimed by these same tenants. Where would the misfits, bums, winos, junkies and creeps live if it were not for slums and slum landlords? Maybe next door to you. These people have to exist. They cannot be eliminated by laws, urban renewal, or do-gooders.

Several years ago, the honorable city fathers of Rochester, New York cleaned skid row of its fleabag hotels, soup kitchens, missions and cheap bars with a bulldozer and federal funds. Skid row, known as Front Street, was in a nonprominent section near the river. As officials cut ribbons and patted themselves ceremoniously on the back, the bums, drunks, and bar owners were busy setting up a new skid row less than a mile away. The new skid row opened on West Main Street three blocks from City Hall, clearly visible to the city's visitors. An excellent example of trying to solve an unsolvable problem with government bureaucracy.

There is a story that makes the rounds every Christmas season about some kid who was born in a stable. Seems that his parents tried to get a room at the inn, but it was booked up for a Kiwanis convention or something like that. So the innkeeper, obviously a slumlord, rented the stable to the carpenter and his pregnant wife. This is where the kid was born.

Slumlords have been with us for more than 2,000 years. Slumlords will always be with us, and, if they were not, bums would be coming to your good units, moving in, driving out your good tenants, and destroying your investment.

Back to Landlords

Although landlords may be second only to prostitutes in being harassed by laws, bureaucrats, and dogooders, I think owning property is the greatest profession in the world. I have been a race car driver, artist, machinist, designer, trucker, and have tried several other occupations and professions; being a landlord is the easiest job I've had. It is one of the few jobs where you get paid when you are not working, or even thinking about working. You get paid twenty-four hours a day, 7 days a week, 365 days a year. You get paid while you are out on a boat, chasing a lover, drinking, or traveling. You set your own hours. Your income is unlimited. If you are a landlord, never give it up. If you are not yet a landlord, now is an excellent time to get started.

All sorts of government rules and regulations can get in your way. Zoning rules say you can only have a certain number of units to house a certain number of people. Plumbing and building codes dictate what materials the buildings can be made of. Assessors decide how much money they will grab for the city. Landmark societies, run by little old ladies who want things to remain as they were in the "good old days," will try to prevent you from tearing down an old porch to build a patio and add a hot tub for that nice, sexy tenant with the 44Ds in apartment 105.

There are numerous other groups of busybodies who will try to get in your way. My advice is to live with them, ignore them, or step on them. Don't ever let them stop you. For every rotten regulation or group, there is one good one that will benefit you. The federal government will allow you depreciation on your investment; operating expenses and taxes are deductible. Almost every city has grants and programs that will benefit landlords. Federal and state funds are available for energy conservation improvements. There are even grants that will pay a landlord for not doing some things. God bless America!

Qualifications for Being a Landlord

Qualifications for being a landlord are

Landlords I Have Known

You may have noticed that there were no qualifications listed for being a landlord. Printing error or editing error? No! There are absolutely no qualifications for being a landlord. No experience is necessary. Anyone can become a landlord.

I met a wise lady who was ninety years old, did not speak English (her tenants did), and managed a building her husband left her. She did an excellent job. I have sold apartments to a couple who looked like Ma and Pa Kettle and had a book under their arm on how to make a million bucks with apartments. They were straight from the farm. Today they are back on the farm—with two Cadillacs, an airplane, and thoroughbred horses. I have sold apartments to a client who would buy only wood frame buildings, never brick. Many of them mysteriously burned and the client was arrested and charged with arson. I have had timid people, rich people, smart people, dumb people, people of all races, tough people, crazy people, and people of every size and shape buy apartment houses. They all had the same chance at success. Some made it. Some didn't. The only thing that made some successful and some failures was how they *trained* their tenants and whether they had a positive mental attitude.

Observations About Landlords

- Have you ever seen a favorable article in the media about a landlord?
- How many times have you heard of a landlord being killed or assaulted by a tenant? Have you heard of a landlord killing a tenant?
- Have you heard a landlord say he was going broke but in the next breath offer to buy your property?
- A landlord who tries to please his tenants' whims usually loses them to a landlord who does nothing to please them.
- A landlord who supplies a turkey at Thanksgiving and a ham at Easter has more vacancies than one who never gives the tenant anything.
- A landlord who keeps the rent low to bribe his "good" tenants to stay has complaints from them about every little item.
- When the landlord supplies the utilities, doors are left open and lights are left on. When the tenants pay the utilities, the doors are closed and the apartment is dark.

2. The Tenant

What is a tenant? The dictionary defines a *tenant* as "one who rents from a landlord."

This is indeed a simple definition. Let's dig a little deeper. Where do they come from? Another planet? At times I have considered sending them to another planet. Most tenants are *born* tenants. They are the children of tenants. Their parents paid rent each and every month. On the first of the month the man in a black suit, with a sneer, a handlebar moustache, and a black top hat arrived at the door. His was a feared knock, especially when the parents did not have all the rent money. As the landlord, he was despised. Sometimes the whole family would hide and be quiet, hoping he would think no one was home and go away. This scene was part of the growing-up and learning cycle of the future tenants.

When these apprentice tenants grew up and married other tenants' children, they followed in their parents' footsteps and rented an apartment. Now they are certified, full-grown tenants. Ninety-nine percent *never* considered buying a home or apartment house, although with FHA, VA, and other programs, most of these tenants were financially qualified to become homeowners. It was not in their make-up to become home-owners. You can't change the spots on a leopard. They were born tenants and most will probably remain tenants.

Other Reasons for Being a Tenant

Bad credit—Although the born tenant usually possesses this qualification, many others become tenants because they cannot manage money and thus have credit problems. These problems eliminate any chance of obtaining a mortgage on a home.

Alcoholics—Again, many born tenants possess this problem, but many tenants, who are drunks, cannot hold jobs, or maintain their dwelling, so they drift from apartment to apartment. Drug users are in this same class.

Irresponsibles—This type absolutely does not want the responsibility of home ownership. These tenants could not take the time from their bowling league or TV football to cut the grass or paint the porch. They do not want responsibility of any kind. Most have the same attitude on their job.

Temporary—These tenants are working in the area for two to three months or going to school. This is probably the only legitimate excuse for being a tenant. However, if the person is going to be in the area one year or more, he is irresponsible if he does not buy a home. In one year the home would appreciate in value. Add this to the rent saved and you have a large sum.

It all boils down to the fact that all of your tenants are either going to be children of tenants who have an inherited hate for landlords, people with rotten credit, drunks, irresponsibles, or people who are going to move out in three months. Not a pretty picture but don't let it worry you. Your best bet is to own several types of units from high-class, luxury units (ideal for temporaries and students) through the spectrum to slums so that you can accommodate the drunks and druggies. If a drunk appears at your luxury unit, you can divert him to your slum and if a temporary appears at your slum, you can shift him to your nice units. No loss of tenant or rent will then occur.

Evaluation of Potential Tenants

After a while you will be able to spot the trouble-makers and undesirables right away. First impressions are usually correct. In the beginning you may ask a few questions which will bring out the potential trouble spots. For example:

(Q) Why are you moving?
(A) The landlord won't fix anything! (This answer may indicate that the tenant is a complainer. Poke around some more. What wouldn't he fix? Who broke it?)

(Q) How long were you living there?
(A) One year. (He may rent from you that long but if the answer is one month, it may indicate a tenant who jumps from place to place.)

(Q) How much rent did you pay at the last place?
(A) $275. (If this is more than your rent, the tenant may be in financial hot water and looking for cheap rent. Ask all the questions that you want. Don't be afraid to pry or embarrass them. By being tenants, they have given up their right to privacy.)

Having invested your time and money in a rental property, you will want to rent to tenants who are not destructive, overly noisy, or chronically late paying their rent. Although there is no way to guarantee that the tenant you select will be reliable, there are precautions you can take to protect your interests.

When a prospective tenant contacts you, you may ask him or her any questions that legitimately pertain to his or her ability to be a good tenant. Do not hesitate to ask anything that may help you to make up your mind. If the prospective tenant is a woman with a black eye, ask if her husband did it. She may have been separated recently and have a violent husband who will knock her door down or otherwise destroy your property.

You may ask for personal references, for the names and addresses of previous landlords, for the applicant's place and length of employment, and amount and source of income. Have him or her fill out an application as per the sample on the next page. Keep this and note anything else you may observe, such as license number and make of car, whom they receive mail from, or bills from a health club or department store. This will help if you ever have to look for them to collect a judgement against them.

You may turn down an applicant if information from these inquiries reveals that he or she would not be likely to pay the rent and preserve your property. *Federal laws absolutely prohibit rental discrimination based on a tenant's race.* I continue to rent to every race imaginable and I have found that no one ethnic group has the distinction of yielding the worst tenants. My property ranges from the grandiose to the ghetto and I have found one thing that does not work— mixing races in the same location. If you put one race on the first floor and another race on the second, you will have problems, especially if they speak different languages. Their ethnic backgrounds prevent them from blending together. Fights and bickering will undoubt-

APARTMENT SIZE REQUIRED

☐ Studio
☐ 1 Bedroom
☒ 2 Bedroom
☐ Other _____

RENTAL APPLICATION

CAR IS 79 FORD LIC# ML 3115 BI WHITE

DATE *MAY 8th 80*

NAME *HELEN BRACE*   PHONE NUMBER *482-3274*

PRESENT ADDRESS *29 KINGSTON ST*

HOW LONG AT THIS ADDRESS? *1 YR*   REASON FOR MOVING? *HOUSE SOLD*

NAME and PHONE NUMBER OF PRESENT LANDLORD *ROB ANDERSEN JR* *586-4700*

PREVIOUS ADDRESS *14 W. MAIN ST*   HOW LONG? *2 YRS*

NAME OF LANDLORD? *GEO. WILLMONT*

PLACE OF EMPLOYMENT *KODAY*   YOUR POSITION *MAINT*   HOW LONG? *5 YR*

NAME OF SUPERVISOR *G. KOTARY*   INCOME PER WEEK *216 00*

WHAT BANKS DO YOU DO BUSINESS WITH? *MARINE MIDLAND*

CREDIT REFERENCES:

1. *M/M ACT 560-106-477-2*
2. *LINCOLN ACT 071-717-141*
3. *GMAC 411-07-1285*
4. _____

PERSONAL REFERENCES and PHONE NUMBER:

1. *T. RICE   716-0181*
2. *Bob DEEGAN   545-7620*
3. *Tom Brace (315)-561-2125*
4. _____

MARITAL STATUS? *DIV.*   NO. of CHILDREN *2*   AGES *5, 7*

FULL NAME OF PERSONS TO OCCUPY PREMISES *HELEN, DAVID, DON*

PETS *NONE*

You have my permission to contact above references in regard to my rental application and if I am accepted I will provide security deposit and sign 1 year lease. I will limit the number of occupants to number specified above.

SIGNED: *H. Brace*

WITNESS: *Andy Kane*

Return the application by mail or in person to:

Andy Kane Realty Corporation
1942 E. Main Street
Rochester, New York 14609

edly occur. As circus people say, "Don't put lions and tigers in the same cage." If at all possible, separate the races. They will be happier and so will you. You may even save lives.

Unless you are renting out rooms in your own home or renting out half of a two-family house occupied by you, you may not discriminate according to color, creed, religion, national origin, sex, marital status, or physical disability.

It is also illegal to refuse to rent to an otherwise suitable tenant because he or she has children, if the space and design of your apartment is adequate for more than one person.

If you don't want children, and many landlords don't, you may avoid hassles by reducing the size of your units in your ad. If you have a three bedroom, it will be attractive to families with three or four dirty brats. Advertise it as a two bedroom and you will probably attract a husband and wife with one grown kid or two professionals. Keep the price the same as a three bedroom.

Many landlords are apprehensive about renting to tenants whose income comes from public assistance. I am not. While there is no law stating that you must rent to welfare clients if you do not wish to, you may find that there are some advantages that you have not considered.

For instance, in some cases you can get a security agreement or deposit from the welfare department assuring that you will get an amount up to one month's rent if the tenant damages your property or leaves without paying. Check with the local welfare department for their policy.

Occasionally you can even arrange with the welfare department to have the rent money sent directly to you.

Remember that it is advisable for you to be as cautious about checking the references of welfare recipients as you would with other prospective tenants. I would even check a little more carefully, since if you have to get a judgement against a working tenant you *may* collect. With a tenant who is on welfare, a judgement may be uncollectable. If the welfare tenant offers you one of their children in lieu of rent, don't take it. Those kids eat too much.

Keep in mind that applicants may try to deceive you. They may only bring one kid and let you assume that is all they have, when they really have six. They may use another person's name or identification, they may overstate their income, or use other tricks. Stay alert; they are out to screw you. It is you against them. You have the advantage. Keep it that way. That's the American way. God bless America!

3. Repairs and the Landlord

Repairs that I am speaking of in this chapter are minor repairs, such as changing a lock, window glass, fuses, faucet washers, electric fixtures, light switches, etc. Not by any means am I suggesting that you stop everything to put in a new furnace, build a chimney, or rebuild a porch. Major repairs like these may not fit into your schedule, but if they do and you can really save bucks, go ahead. Minor repairs are the ones I suggest you make on the spot.

Let's take a simple example. The tenant informs me that the kitchen faucet is running (or the bathroom faucet or toilet). My new Cadillac Eldorado with white leather upholstery, air conditioning, stereo, and everything available to waste gas is parked at the curb. I am dressed in my custom-made $400 suit. I have two choices:

A) I can call "Johnny the plumber" who will come over tomorrow and install a five-cent washer. The water will run until he does. If it is the hot water faucet, and it usually is, the hot water heater will turn on several times. For this small job, he will charge me at least an hour's wage, $40 to $50, and I will be paying for wasted water and energy for the water heater. This is the way most landlords would handle the problem.

B) I can open the trunk of my Cadillac, reach into my well-equipped tool box, and get a pair of pliers, pipe wrench, screw driver, and washer. I'm going to get my hands dirty, but in the trunk I also have paper towels and hand cleaner. I do this job in about ten minutes. No plumber, no wasted water or energy, no wasted money. The tenant is instantly happy. Even if I get my $400 suit dirty, I can get it cleaned for $5. Savings: about $50.

The Tool Box

You should have a well-equipped tool box in your trunk at all times. The first time you do an emergency repair, you will save the cost of the tool box. You should have:

Tool box	Wire cutters
Pipe wrench	Tin snips
Pliers	Tape measure
Screw driver	Paper, pen
Electrical tape	Hack saw
Utility knife	Washers
Hammer	Fuses
Staple gun	Screws
Toilet parts	Nails
Locks, lock parts	

Your tool box can be assembled by using duplicates of tools that you have around the house, or purchasing them at a discount store. When you purchase them, don't buy junk. A tool is an important item; buy only the best. Cheap tools will not do the job and will be a waste of money.

Major Repairs

Always question major repairs. When some flunkie furnace man tells you "The furnace is shot," don't panic. Seldom is a furnace really shot. What does this jerk know anyway? If he was smart, he would be a landlord, not a dirty furnace repair man. Ask him *exactly* what is wrong. Have him show you. Don't be in a hurry. Even if it is ten degrees below zero outside and six tenants are standing there screaming, take your time. Consider the problem.

Is it 10 April and nearly the end of the heating season? Can you get someone to patch it up? Are you going to sell the dump in the spring? Get another repairman to give you his opinion. I had one creep of a furnace man tell me the furnace was a hazard, leaking carbon monoxide (it was!) and making a gas chamber out of the building. He said I should put in a new furnace immediately. I didn't. I called another furnace monkey and he cleaned the chimney for $50. This furnace is still working today, five years later. Never trust a repairman. They are as rotten and dishonest as tenants. In fact, you will probably find that they are someone's tenants.

Learn as much as you can about the operation of furnaces, hot water heaters, electric systems, and plumbing systems. It will save you bucks in the long run.

Prices

Every tradesman has different goals and overhead. Some want to get rich today. Some will be happy just to feed their ten illegitimate kids. Prices on a $3,000 job may vary by $1,000. That's a good hunk of dough. If you take three extra hours to get three estimates, and you find one a grand lower, you made $333 per hour for your time. Be sure estimates are written, include a completion date and show an itemized list of what is being done, and be sure the contractor is insured.

Don't give him a dime until the job is done. If he wants money up front, tell him no. I never pay until the job is done to my satisfaction, and then I wait awhile. If it is a gutter or roof job, don't pay until after the first rain storm. You will be surprised how fast a contractor will come back to fix a roof or gutter leak when he hasn't got his money yet.

If you get three estimates from contractors and one is $800, one is $1,000, and one is $1,500, the guy with the $800 is obviously a butcher and incompetent and would foul up the whole building if he tried to work on it. I'll show you how to get the $1,000 guy to do the job for $800. Call him back. Tell him you liked him (or his work on his last job) but he is $200 over the other guy. He doesn't know the other guy is a butcher. Tell him he can have the job if he can do it for $800. Show him the $800 estimate so he doesn't think you are deceiving him. Nine out of ten times he will go for it.

Under the Table

You call the plumbing company and they send one of their workers to do a job for you. He looks at it and says, "Parts and labor—$200." Ask him how long it will take. Maybe he can do it on his lunch hour for $100, all cash to him, tax free. Remember, most tradesmen are tenants and that puts them in the dishonest category. Tell him you will call the plumbing company and tell them the price is too high, that they should forget it, or that the problem corrected itself. He can get right to work and make himself a fast $100. Again, nine out of ten times, you will have a deal. Give it a try.

Barter

Do you have a tenant who is a plumber, heating mechanic or other tradesman? Give him a week's free rent to do the repairs. It will reduce your taxable income and the tenant will make a buck. If the job is worth $100, pay him $50 in free rent. Never give him $100 in rent for a $100 job. Insist on a price first. Don't let him go to sleep on the job and take five hours for a ten-minute job. Barter is becoming a common way in the United States to cheat the tax man. Take advantage of it. That's the American way. God bless America!

4. Rent — The Fruits of Your Labor

Rent is the goal of nearly every investor-landlord. I say nearly all because some people actually invest in real estate as a tax shelter and are not looking toward profit. One thing you must remember is that if you do not get that rent each and every month, you are heading down the road to financial disaster. At all costs, you must get *all* the rent out of *every* tenant by any and all means.

You have probably read of infectious diseases spreading like wildfire when unchecked (plague and VD, for example). The same will happen with nonpayment of rent. If you allow the thief in Apt. 1-A to get away without paying March rent, he will brag and spread the word that he beat the landlord out of March rent. In April this will definitely spread to 1-B, 2-B, 5-A, and on and on. Obviously if 1-A is not paying, why should they?

You should get on this cheat's case immediately (see chapter on eviction) to show that in your property the policy is "No pay, no stay."

How Much Rent?

There is no set way of determining how much to charge for your units except where rent control is in effect. You can add all expenses, estimates of vacancies and repairs, reserves for replacement and other factors, and desired profits, to arrive at a rental figure. If this figure is more than what other units in the same area are renting for, you will have vacancies and unrentable units. No formula will work regardless of what you have heard or read in the how-to-become-a-millionaire books.

The only method is to "Charge what the traffic will bear." This is established by consulting the classified ads for similar apartments and their rents. You may even be wise to visit the vacant apartments and see how they compare. This will be good information to have when showing prospective tenants your apartment. You can overcome objections with such statements as, "Yes, ours are $15 per month more than Smith Arms because electricity is included here and we have off-street parking."

Do Not Under-Rent

Many older and beginning landlords keep rents low to avoid vacancies. This is crazy. For example: Rent is $200 per month but should be $225. Your loss over a year is $300. If you raise the rent and the tenant moves, you would have to have this unit vacant for *six weeks* to actually lose money. If you have five apartments in this building that are under-rented by $25 each, you have a $1,500 annual loss. Get the rents up. Keep them at market value at all times.

How to Raise Rents

Completely disregard the tenants' circumstances. It is irrelevant that they are sick, crippled, old, blind, on a pension, on welfare, or unemployed. You are in business to make a profit—period. There are various agencies of the local government, federal government and religious orders in business to take care of these unfortunate tenants. They will always be taken care of by some do-gooder organization that is probably operating on your tax money anyway, so your conscience should be clear.

I have had hundreds of these tenants try to intimidate me for raising their rents to market value. I *never* knuckled under. Many moved and I think that nearly all of them rented an apartment that was priced the same, or even more, than the new rent I was asking. Analyze the rents for the area and set a rent for your unit. Inform tenants in writing similar to the sample.

Follow this sample exactly. *Every word* has been analyzed for results, as you will see in the following: *"Dear* _____ *"*—Fill in the blank by hand with the tenant's name. This gives the feeling that the notice is impersonal and many other tenants are also getting it.

Dear __Mr. Joshe__

        Due to the increased cost of insurance, taxes, maintenance, and other costs beyond my control, the rent for the unit you occupy will be $ __356 00__, effective on __11-1-81__.

        If you will be moving, please give 30 days written notice.

        Sincerely,

        Andy Kane
        Owner

"Due to the increased cost of . . ."—This takes you off the hook and makes a villain out of the gas company, insurance company, and tax man. Every red-blooded American hates these guys anyway.

"Rent for the apartment you occupy will be $_____."—Again fill in by hand for the impersonal form letter approach.

"Effective on _____*"*—This should be the shortest period of time allowed by law. Check your laws. My reasoning is that tenants are lazy by nature. If you give them too long, they may look for an apartment and find one. If the time period is short, they will wait awhile and it will be too late to find anything before the rent increase. Once they begin paying the new higher rent, they will get used to it and adjust their life style to afford it (one less night bowling or two less six-packs a week).

"If you are moving . . ."—This is one of the most important sentences in the letter. It is a no-nonsense statement that will take the wind out of any moving threat. You are telling them in advance, "Go ahead and move. I don't give a damn. You can't scare me!"

"Give 30 days written notice"—Be sure all communications and applications are *written* notices. When they *tell* you in person that they are moving, say "O.K." and drop it right away. On the day they move and you go over to check the apartment and get their key, they will be expecting their security deposit. Don't give it to them. Insist that they told you only a few days ago that they were moving, not thirty days ago. It's their word against yours. They never gave you *written* notice, so you just made some easy money. The first time you keep one security deposit because you read this book, you will have paid for the cost of the book and made

money besides. If you feel guilty, you can send the extra money to me.

"*Sincerely,* _____, *Owner*"—Don't write "landlord." "Owner" will create the least animosity. Hand-deliver notices to each tenant or mail them. Certified or registered mail works well, because you can verify that the tenant received the notice. It also costs more money and, if you have a lot of units, it can add up. I send them by first class mail. In all my years I have had only one tenant claim he did not receive his notice. But I fixed him by sending a duplicate notice for an amount $10 per month more than the first one. Would you believe that all of a sudden the tenant called and told me that the first notice miraculously turned up?

How Often to Raise Rents

I do it every year. Expenses usually go up on everything during twelve months. Good barometers are a loaf of bread and a six-pack of beer. These are two items that reflect very clearly the percentage of increase in your area. Keep track of the percentage of increase over one year and use that percentage to increase your rents. I feel that one raise per year is sufficient, but I also raise rents whenever there is a change of tenants. If you have a wise guy who is a trouble maker, you may want to raise the rent every month.

Play it by ear but don't get into a rut of allowing tenants to pay the same rent for years. Everything in this country goes up in price. Keep your rentals on the red, white, and blue inflation bandwagon. That's the American way. God bless America!

Rent Control

It has been said that the best way to destroy a city is to bomb it, and the second best way to destroy a city is to establish rent controls. Rent controls absolutely do not work. It is not possible to limit the amount a landlord can charge for rent, while all other operating expenses are not controlled. If the cost of utilities, insurance, wages, interest, supplies, repairs and other items necessary to the operation of an apartment are escalating and rents are frozen, the landlord has only one choice: to defer maintenance and repairs, delay tax and mortgage payments, and reduce services to the tenants. This means that the property will deteriorate and possibly become a slum or be abandoned. Most of the slums in major cities were created by do-gooders who initiated rent controls.

Some Solutions

Band together and fight the controls. They are discriminating. They are harassing one category of businessman. If the tenants must be protected from the landlord to survive, is it not necessary to protect them also from the butcher, banker, gas station operator, and even their minister? There should be hamburger controls, interest controls, gas price controls, and minister controls (if you attend church, you have heard the minister's Sunday pitch for more bucks in the collection).

Sound ridiculous? It's no more ridiculous than controlling rents. I believe that rent controls deprive a landlord of his property without due process. Fight it all the way. Don't give up.

A Temporary Solution

This will help you temporarily if you feel the government is about to start rent control in your area. It's used by all the car manufacturers. Have you ever wondered why Ford, G.M., Chrysler and even the imports offer $500, $1,000, or $1,200 rebates? Why not just reduce the price of the car? The reason is that they are afraid of price controls. By keeping the selling price artificially high and giving you back the difference in the form of a rebate, they have a hedge against a future price freeze. If there is one, they simply reduce or eliminate the rebate.

You can do the same thing with your rents. If an apartment rents for $250, rent it for $300 with the understanding that you will give the tenants back $50 when they pay their rent. (Make this agreement verbally.) If price controls are enforced, your rent book shows $300 per month. This will help you over the first few months and may give you time to fight the controls.

Obviously if the rebates work for car manufacturers, they should work for you. That's the American way. God bless America!

5. Collecting Rent

There are probably dozens of ways to collect rents. Some tenants mail the rent to you. Some bring it to you. Some pay the superintendent and you get it from him. Some leave it in the apartment and you go in and get it. Some pay an appointed third person. Some pay you in person at the apartment.

All of these methods work to a degree, but the one sure-fire way to collect rent is the last: face-to-face at the apartment. This allows you to see how the tenant is treating your shack. It gives you the feeling of cold, hard cash in your hand which is a rewarding feeling and an incentive to stay in the landlord profession. If, when you collect the rent, you see several big boxes in the corner, you will have an idea that this tenant may be getting ready to move without notice. If you notice that the husband is missing, you may anticipate future financial problems. Looking at the tenant's living conditions definitely helps you plan. Is the apartment going to need paint or repairs soon? Are faucets dripping? Drains plugged? Visual inspection is the only way. Other methods have glaring disadvantages.

Check in the Mail

It may get lost. You won't get it until the third, and since you regularly expect it on the third, if it does not arrive, you give it another day or two. After all, you reason, the tenant has been there a year and always pays on time. You call on the fifth and get an operator who says, "What number did you call?" You drive over and when you knock on the door, it sounds different. That's because a room without furniture echoes. That's right, the nice tenant has pulled out without notice and you didn't know until the sixth. Even if you rent it that day, you lose one-fourth the monthly rental. If you had known on the first, you could have hung out a "For Rent" sign and grabbed a live one without any loss of rent.

You say you had a security deposit? Big deal. They probably did some damage and that's what security deposits are for, not to use as rent. Collect in person each and every month!

Bring It to You

Do you want a steady stream of filthy tenants in broken down cars driving up to your palace? Certainly not. This will give them an open invitation to come over and complain whenever they want—like at your family picnic, with all your in-laws and friends present, when a 250-pound, unshaven slob in a dirty undershirt, with a can of cheap beer in his hand, walks in and tells you his toilet does not work and you should fix it now.

Bringing rent to your place is also a security risk. You have fifteen slobs bringing $225 each to your place. Each of them knows that the others bring you cash and, as stupid as they are, they multiply $225 x 15 and get $3,375. For that amount of money most tenants would kill, and they may kill you or your whole family. Don't encourage them. Never allow them to come to your residence.

Bring It to the Superintendent

One of the surest ways I know of to part a landlord from his money is to allow a middleman to come between him and his rent. *Never* have a superintendent collect rent, not under any circumstances, not even if the superintendent has been there twenty-five years. He can't be trusted. He is basically a tenant and a tenant can't be trusted. You are also endangering this old fool by letting him handle large sums of cash. This thief is living in a den of thieves and they know he has cash on the first of the month. If the superintendent doesn't steal it, the other tenants will. They may also whack this old geezer in the head in the process and the blood will stain your carpet.

Third Person

There is a big bruiser who collects rent for you; why does he do this? You pay him 10 percent to collect your rent. Ninety-five percent of your tenants will pay anyway. This bum will collect the gravy rents—the 95 percent—take his 10 percent commission, and leave you with the 5 percent who are hard to collect from. Why do you need this bum to do the easy work when you have to chase the 5 percent that are hard cases? Do the entire rent collecting yourself. In all my years collecting rent, I have resorted to having someone else collect rent only *once*. I had a broken shoulder and was confined. A friend of mine had a heart attack on the twentieth of the month and was confined to the hospital. Would you believe, he had a miraculous recovery on the thirtieth and collected his rent on the first. That's a true landlord!

Our Route

Never, never establish a route or schedule for collecting rents. I collect rents anywhere between 6 A.M. and 7 P.M. My property is scattered over an entire city. I start on the east and work west one month, west to east another, in the middle and go both ways the next month. If a tenant is going to ambush me, he will have to spend some time waiting.

In my real estate business, I was showing a rooming house to a prospective buyer. I contacted the owner and he told me to bring the buyer at 11 A.M. Saturday. "I always go there at 11 A.M. to collect the rent," he said. I told this owner my theory about collection at the same time each week or month. He told me he had been doing it for twenty years without problems. About two weeks later, I read that he had been stabbed and robbed by one of his ex-tenants at exactly 11 A.M. on a Saturday morning. You may get away with it for a while but don't take a chance.

The Right to Bear Arms

The Constitution guarantees it. The antigun movement tries to take your right away. How many antigun nuts are landlords? I don't think these crusaders are out collecting rents. They are probably eight to five factory Joes. If you get killed by a tenant with a gun, they will use your death as ammunition for their "ban the handgun" cause. They won't consider the fact that your tenant's gun was unlicensed and illegal. Protect your right to have a weapon. Buy one, learn how to use it, keep it in top working order, and hope you never have to use it.

The kind of gun you buy is irrelevent, but let me give you some tips. A .25 caliber automatic will fit in your pocket. You can carry it anywhere anytime. It will stop a tenant or mugger with ease. The pros use them; take a tip from the pros. A .25 caliber is only accurate for a short distance, but you are not going to shoot anyone a block away. You are going to use it on a mugger close enough to take your money. I have had friends who bought pearl-handled, chrome-plated six-shooters like Wyatt Erp's. They dragged them around a week, then left them home because they were big and uncomfortable. Get a small gun and carry it everywhere, especially when collecting rents. Be sure you abide by all laws in your area regarding registering and carrying this gun. Use caution when children are in the family.

Warning Tenants

When I first rent to a tenant, I take the gun out nonchalantly with my money and make change. I let them know by this method that I am armed. It discourages them from considering me an easy target.

Easy Money

Do you want to make some easy money? Your tenant may not have the ability to count money and he may pay you too much. If you count it in front of him, he may note the mistake. Have you ever noticed the signs near cash registers that state "Count your change before leaving"? Do you think that business gives a damn if you are short changed? Absolutely not. They are afraid that you will walk out with some of their money. Most mistakes are made in your favor, both in stores and by tenants.

When a tenant pays, place the money directly in your right pocket. Keep this pocket empty of other items or money. As soon as you are outside the tenant's door, take it out and count it. If it is short, immediately knock on the door and yell at this no good crook. If there is too much, forget it. You deserve it. I guarantee that this practice will net you an extra hundred or so each year—tax free! Get all you can. That's the American way. God bless America!

6. More Money

This makes everybody happy! Even millionaires' eyes light up at these words. Money, money, money! That's what it's all about. If you ever meet anyone who says he has all the money he needs, shun him. He's a loser and losing is contagious. His ridiculous thinking may spread to you and destroy your positive, greedy attitude.

Let's assume you have your rents up to top market value for your units. All units are rented, you are getting maximum profits out of your investment. Right? Wrong!

You can still get more bucks out of the slobs who are living there. Here's how.

The tenant pays his own gas, electric, and heat, which is oil. Contact an oil company other than the one the tenant is using. Ask him if he will give you a penny a gallon on each new customer you bring him, and also provide emergency service, without charge, on the burner unit. If one company says no, shop around. Try small dealers who are building a business. When you find one who is receptive, contact your tenant and tell him he must buy oil from "XXX Oil Company" because they are providing you with burner service. Do the same with every tenant who uses oil. Depending on your holdings, this "penny a gallon" may easily pay for your vacation this winter. Isn't that nice? Your tenants are sending you to sunny Florida as a bonus.

Even though tenants are subhuman, they use most of the products we humans require: milk, groceries, and meat. Make arrangements with a milkman, similar to those made with the oil man. Tell the meat market and grocery (small Mom/Pop stores are easiest) that you would like to bring in a new customer. In return you want a roast or case of beer. Take your new tenant in and introduce him to the grocery store owner, and enjoy your Sunday roast at the expense of your lame-brain tenant.

Cars, appliances, snow mobiles, and TVs are attractive to tenants. They spend on these flashy items. Cultivate salesmen in all of these lines and tell your tenants that you have "connections" so they should call you before they make a major purchase. If they are going to waste their dough on these frivolous items, you might as well get a few bucks.

Or ask your lawyer to handle your next closing for free, if you send him a few new clients. Take your ex-con tenant, who just got picked up for child molesting, to see your legal whiz. Tenants, due to their being basically unreliable and dishonest, have the biggest need for lawyers. Your lawyer will get plenty of work from your rotten tenants. Your next closing will be paid for by the tenants.

Your insurance covers your building for fire, liability, and other risks, but *does not* cover the tenants' possessions. Ninety-nine percent of these idiots think that if a fire occurs, *your* insurance will replace their broken-down davenport and second-hand clothes. This is not true. For them to have coverage on their possessions, they must have a tenant's or renter's policy. This will also cover them for personal liability and while on vacations.

Contact your agent, or any independent agent, and ask him what he will do for you if you bring him a number of new clients. Always use an independent agent. He can wheel and deal because he's in business for himself, just as you are. Independent agents are listed in the Yellow Pages under their own heading. If they say that the most they can give you is a fiver because state law restricts what they can give, tell them they can take you and your beautiful wife out to dinner at the best restaurant in town or slip you a nice, clean, crisp twenty.

Your tenants will be surprised to find out that their worthless furnishings are not covered by your insurance. The best way to inform them, and to sell them on your agent, is a letter worded like this:

WARNING, WARNING!

Our insurance covers only the building you occupy! Your possessions are not covered!
In the event of a fire, you would not receive one cent from us for your valuable possessions.
You should obtain coverage on your clothing, valuables and furniture immediately! Contact
Westcott Insurance at 235-1400 immediately!

Andy Kane

Andy Kane, Owner

Don't change a word of it (except your agent's name and number). It's designed to work. "Warning, warning" and "in the event of fire" will scare the hell out of them. They might even think that you sent the letter to protect yourself because you are contemplating arson to make a fast buck. "Your valuable possessions," "clothing," and "valuables," will make their crooked minds spring into action. "If there was a fire, I could claim that my wife lost the diamond earrings that she wears when we go to the opera," they will think.

"Contact Westcott Insurance at 235-1400" is an order. Remember that tenants are used to taking orders and they are lazy. You are giving them an order and a phone number, so they don't have to look in the phone book. Send the letter and watch the greedy jerks call your agent and insure their worthless junk.

But *watch out.* Check your insurance coverage on any building where the tenant gets a renter's policy. Be sure you have plenty of coverage. If this tenant gets laid off, or is ready to move, he may set his apartment or your building on fire to collect on his junk. I have had this happen. It is not far-fetched. Remember you are dealing with mental midgets when you are dealing with tenants. Be sure your coverage is adequate.

7. Using Tenants For Profit

Have you ever thought of selling your tenants to your friends? Many tenants, due to their job habits, have periods of temporary or prolonged unemployment. They can usually make their rent money through unemployment insurance or welfare handouts. During this time they are available for almost any kind of work you might have, providing they receive cash for payment and can stay on the dole.

Most tenants can cut grass, rake leaves, paint, or clean basements. With a little bit of encouragement (free lunch or a bottle of wine) besides the under-the-table cash, they may even do a fairly good job.

Your friends are expecting to pay $4,000 to have their house painted. You look in your woodpile of tenants, find one whose hand fits the handle of a brush, buy a twenty-five foot extension ladder, some paint and scrapers, and give your friend a bid of $2,500. Since the tenant is being subsidized by unemployment or welfare, he can work cheap. Don't pay him by the hour or the job may take longer than it took to build the pyramids. Pay him $300 per side, when each side is finished. This way you know exactly what the job will cost. Be sure your friend pays you and not the tenant, in cash, of course. He is saving $1,500 so he shouldn't object. Don't put anything in writing or you may end up in jail or, even worse, talking to Uncle Sam's helpers. Just consider the possible breakdown of the $2,500: $1,200 for the tenant (be sure you grab any rent due before you pay him), $200 for a ladder (which you keep), $500 for paint and supplies, and $600 for you. Not a bad profit, since the whole operation probably took only a half-hour of your time.

Apply the same procedure to any task that you can use tenant power for. Let your friends and relatives know that you have the manpower available. Use caution in making any agreements with tenants that they could use against you if they become injured, revengeful, or come under the scrutiny of the I.R.S.

I heard of a novel solution to the liability problem which also increased the tenant's productivity. Business

INTERIOR
EXTERIOR

FREE ESTIMATES
REPAIRS

• MACLIN PAINTING •
1328 E. MAIN ST.

CHARLES MACLIN, PRES.
ANDY KANE, SALES MGR.

392-4234

cards were printed up with the tenant's name as president and the tenant's address. The landlord was listed as sales manager and the landlord's phone number was used on the card.

Since the tenant was "obviously" the president and owner of this thriving business and the tenant himself passed out most of the cards, there was little chance that, if the tenant broke his neck, he could come back on the landlord who was listed as a salesman. This tenant-landlord business lasted several years. The landlord simply took the calls, looked at the job, and took half the profit.

The tenant was busy most of the time and not loafing around the landlord's property using lights and water. He learned a trade, if you can call painting a trade, and elderly homeowners saved considerable money. This landlord helped keep America beautiful and made money doing it.

There is a hell of a lot more money to be made from your tenants than just the rent. If you don't get it, someone else will. If God wanted them to be rich, they would have been born landlords instead of tenants. Take their money. It's the American way—God bless America!

8. The Eviction

As was stated earlier, I do not recommend any tactics that may violate the law. I will give you a few ideas for removal of unwanted tenants and relate several instances that may help you train remaining tenants in a building.

Ninety-nine percent of the times an eviction is necessary, it is due to unpaid rent. Let's consider this in more depth. When a tenant owes you $250 rent and does not pay, he is stealing, in my opinion. You need this money to make good your obligations, and when it is not paid, you must use personal funds to pay your bills. You have not received your $250, plus you have had to throw in $250 of your hard-earned money to make the mortgage or utility payments. You have been *robbed* of $500 by this rotten tenant.

If he had accosted you on the street with a black mask and gun and taken $500, you could have him arrested for violating the law. You could use deadly force to stop him. You would be a hero if you did stop him and the world would be on your side.

But, he has robbed you semilegally and you will be the villain in the eyes of the world. It's not right or fair, but that's how it is.

Since the tenant is not playing fair, should you? If you want to play fair, call your legal whiz and start his time clock. After several court appearances and much time and cash, you *may* obtain (depending on sympathy of the judge, the stormy weather, the tenant's alibi, or the tenant's kids) an eviction warrant which will enable you to hire a mover, at your expense, and place the tenant's broken-down furniture in storage, also at your expense. You will be entitled to hire a marshal or officer of the court who will remove the tenant himself.

All this may take two months and you will not receive rent for this period. The best you can hope for is that you will be granted a judgment for the rent

and eviction expenses. This judgment is then filed with the court in the *hope* that someday this deadbeat will pay you. This legal way will take time and money and be very aggravating to say the least.

Remember, this tenant is trying to rob you and is definitely not playing fair. Why not fight fire with fire? I do not admit to doing any of the following, but I was a first-hand observer of the events.

For example, you have a tenant whom you want to remove. Reason is unimportant. You want them out! There are three approaches you can use.

The Soft Approach

Don't be nice. If you continue to be as nice as you were when they were paying rent, they will have no incentive to seek other shelter. Be rotten, abusive, mean, disrespectful, loud, belligerent, and threaten to do physical harm and violence. Make repeated trips to the property several times a day at odd hours. Harass the tenant, scream and yell. Be sure liquor is on your breath. Don't get drunk and go over, just have one drink, so the tenant smells the booze. The effect is what you want. People are always more afraid of drunks. If you don't drink, slosh some liquor around in your mouth and spit it out (preferably on the tenant's shoe). This will give you the drunk effect without being inebriated.

Insist that if they don't have their possessions out by Friday, you will have them moved out. Contact a local mover using the tenant's name and request that he come over and give you (the tenant) an estimate on moving five rooms of furniture. He will appear, ask for tenant Jones and say, "I'm here to estimate moving your furniture." This will scare the tenant. He will think that you have hired someone to move him out. He will slam the door on the mover and the mover will leave thinking he was the object of a crank call. It will not cost you a cent. The tenant will probably begin packing on his own. Don't call fire or police departments to harass the tenant. It is illegal to make a false report and someone might be injured by the police car or fire truck responding to the false call.

The Slightly Harder Approach

The tenant has resisted the soft approach, so we must go one more round. I have heard of landlords who obtain a change of address from the post office and fill it in, changing the tenant's address to 1600 Pennsylvania Avenue, Washington, D.C. or the local crazy house. This is, of course, illegal.

The same landlords also called the local phone and utility companies and said they were the tenant and had the phone and utilities shut off. They then placed a classified ad in the local newspaper offering various items of the tenant's furniture for sale: an RCA console color TV, three months old for $125, with the tenant's address, no phone number. Usually fifty people show up to buy the tenant's underpriced possession. They become belligerent when the tenant refuses to sell the item after they have driven over to see it. Some excellent examples of harassment came to light in the recent Hillside Strangler case.

THE STRANGLER CASE

Arizona, Wood testified. ... ... nome to Buono. Wood said he was harassed by Bianchi and Buono.

Wood testified that an advertisement was placed in a newspaper saying he was going out of business (Bianchi said he placed the ad at Buono's urging), his utilities were shut off and telegrams were sent to his old law school classmates telling them he was quitting his practice because of "morals charges" against him.

The harassment stopped after he sent some former clients who were Hell's Angels over to "talk" with Bianchi and Buono, Wood said. The leader was "6 foot 7, about 370 pounds and real ugly" and called Tiny, Wood added.

The grand jury transcripts in the non-m... ... charges ... ...or emb...

The entire purpose of this ploy is to make the tenant *uncomfortable* at this address. Also during this period, all the tactics used in the soft approach are continued, possibly even intensified. If you have an application that they filled out when renting, begin calling relatives and friends they listed. Shout and holler at them that this no-good tenant is wrecking your apartment, is a deadbeat, and since he gave their names when renting, you may name them in a lawsuit. (You really can't.) This will get the tenant's relatives and friends on his back.

All this may take some of your time but it will save you much money. Don't give up if they do not move. Remember they are living free and to give up something free takes motivation.

The Hard Approach

We have not been successful so far, so we must go to the hard approach.

Do you know any big guys? Preferably with tattoos, not much education, poor grammar, leather jackets? Take them to your property and, in the tenants' presence, ask them how much money they want to throw all the furniture out in the street.

Conduct an inspection of the apartment and discuss the items of furniture. Have your big friends say "We'll probably have to break the legs off that table to get it through the door" and other discouraging remarks. Tell the tenants that they have until 3 P.M. on Saturday, or whatever time you decide, to get their possessions out, or your crew will do it for them.

I have found that many tenants will get out on their own at this point. If they don't get out, return at 4 P.M. with your oxes. Why at 4 P.M. instead of 3 P.M.? The tenant may call the police and have them waiting for you at 3 P.M. This will fool them.

Before you begin moving them out, cut or disconnect the phone, if you haven't already done so. You can usually find the wires in the basement. If you don't know a phone line from an electric line, have an electrician point it out. There is usually a terminal block in the basement near where the line enters the property where it's easy to disconnect. Don't cut an electric line by mistake. Remember we are trying to get rid of the tenants, not you! This will prevent them from calling the law while you are assisting them in moving.

Have your guys start the moving. A good way to pack the tenant's things is as follows: Ash trays—leave the ashes in them and put them in the dresser drawers with the clean clothes. Food from refrigerator—ice cream and frozen foods should be packed in with clothing from the closets in big trash bags. Glass, pictures, and mirrors—place those on the ground first so sofa legs don't sink in the soft yard.

Get the idea? Your tenant may help move his possessions himself when your crew starts packing. In this case, give him a one-hour extension to complete the move. If he doesn't begin helping, I finish the job.

What if he calls the cops? No problem. Tell the police the tenant asked you to help him move, told you the truck was coming in half an hour, and that he was paying by the hour for the move. By having everything ready at the curb, he would save money. Insist that this is what happened. When the tenant tells his story, call him a liar, threaten to sue him for slander, and tell him that this is the last time you will ever help him move. It usually works.

Select the crew wisely. One day I had a helper who was carrying one end of a sofa out the door with one of the tenant's crying kids wrapped around his leg. My helper put the sofa down, reached in his pocket, pulled out his wallet and offered to pay the tenant's back rent. Guys like this should be shot. This destroys the effect you want to create. It makes it appear that you were wrong and the tenant is right.

Training Tenants

You can avoid the effort of using these approaches if you train your tenants to behave as you want them to from the beginning. Here is an example of how to get them off on the right foot. You have a six-family unit where three tenants pay on time, two pay a little late, and one is moving. Your goal is to train *all* the tenants to pay their rent on time. Use the:

The No-Eviction Eviction

Tenants are exactly like children with one exception: children grow up. Tenants do not. The tenants who are moving have given notice, the rent is current, and they informed you that they will have everything out of the apartment by 10 A.M. Saturday. You show up at 9:30 A.M. While you are still in the hall outside their apartment, scream "I told you yesterday that I wanted all your stuff out of this damn apartment by 9:30. If you don't have everything out in a half hour, I'll kill you."

These tenants will think you are crazy. What do you care? They're moving anyway. Make an example out of them for the benefit of the other tenants. Quietly enter the apartment and ask them if there is anything they are discarding—an old chair, lamp, or table—and if you can have it. Take this out in the hall and with as much noise as possible, smash it, scream and yell, and kick and throw this chair or lamp or whatever down the stairs and out into the yard. You will notice five other tenants peeking out their windows. Your tenants are now all packed up and ready to go. Keep yelling that they are no good jerks and if you ever see them in the area, you will run over them with your car. As they pull away, chase their car waving your fist, and take a kick at their back bumper. Now go back in and lock up the apartment. Tell the remaining tenants that those deadbeats were two days behind in their rent.

I guarantee that *before* the first of next month rolls around, all the rent from that building will be in. No stragglers. Tenants from that building will be on time. The old tenants will tell new tenants that if they don't pay, "That crazy landlord will throw you out. We saw him do it to the people in 2-A. He chased them right down the street." This is the best public relations effort a landlord can make.

This procedure will work just as well on a single-family dwelling. You must do everything on the front porch in this case so the neighbors hear you. A hot summer night is an excellent time. The neighbors will then tell the next tenant what happened to their predecessor for being late with the rent.

These are just a sampling of techniques that work. I am sure I have your juices flowing and you could add to the list with your ideas. Keep in mind that one bad tenant is like one bad apple. If you don't get him out of your building, he will spoil the whole place.

You are entitled to your rent and tenants shouldn't try to beat you out of it. If they do, kick them out. You can't let them disrupt your business. This country is founded on good business practices and tenants are un-American if they do not pay. God bless America.

9. Tenants and Sex

Let me assure you, both tenants and sex are O.K. kept in their proper places. But if you get sexually involved with your tenants, you are looking for problems.

You may never be approached by a tenant. Look in the mirror. Fat, ugly, bald, old, decrepit you. What broad would want you? You're lucky you got a wife before you fell apart. Now if you were a handsome devil like I am, you could have problems.

If you don't have any desire to grab a tenant, don't think you will ever have the opportunity, and wouldn't even if you did, you may be inclined to skip this chapter. Don't. Sooner or later, fat, ugly, bald old you will be accused of having sex with a tenant, especially if you are married.

Tenants seeking revenge for a rent increase, eviction, or lack of service are inclined to call your wife (or husband if you are a female landlord) and swear they saw you in bed with the sexy tenant in Apt. 7-A. The best way to nip this problem in the bud is to tell your spouse right now that this is going to happen. Tell her that when this call arrives, she can prevent it from reoccurring with a simple statement. When they tell her how you are romancing the young chick in their building,

have her say, "That's O.K. We have an open marriage
and he can do whatever he wants." They will never call
back again. Once they know they can't make trouble for
you in this manner, their ammunition is wet. They must
move on to other ploys to get even with you for the
rent increase.

Let's consider another aspect of your having sex
with a tenant. You looked in the mirror. What tenant
would want you in your decrepit condition? A hard-up
one. If she is hard-up, what's she doing? Probably prop-
ositioning the milk man, oil man, bread man, meter
reader and paper boy. Not having the character and
moral fiber of a landlord, they are probably taking her
up on it too. Her chances of having VD are probably

greater than that of a hooker who is cautious with her clients. Never fool around with a tenant.

My attorney once advised me to never say never. So let's say, "Almost never fool around with a tenant." What if the tenant just left the convent two weeks ago, looks like a starlet, and just can't resist you? Wasn't "Never say never" good advice? You can't let the poor girl suffer any longer. She pays her rent on time. Just this once, you can give in.

Two weeks later when the rent is due, she says, "I'm not paying. I'll tell your wife, if you try to make me pay." Worried? Not you. Your wife will get her call and say, "That's O.K." You can have your cake and eat it too.

You may experience a tenant who, when she is not going to pay her rent, threatens to call the police and say you attacked her or tried to rape her. The best way to avoid this problem is to have someone with you when you collect the rent. Usually you will know a problem tenant in advance. If you can't take someone with you, ask another tenant to go to the apartment with you. Don't ask a tenant who is friendly with the problem tenant or you may end up doing time. Don't enter her apartment or house. Stay outside the door in plain sight.

If she does actually go to the police, tell them the entire story. They are used to false complaints and will confront her with the penalties for filing a false complaint. She will probably withdraw it. You could get her for false arrest, but don't. If your name is dragged through the press with a false arrest case regarding rape, it may damage your credibility in future court cases.

While on the subject of sex, let's talk about homosexual sex. Gays, lesbians, and transvestites make very acceptable tenants. I have rented to homosexuals and most of them respected the property, paid on time, and were professional people (teachers, doctors, and law-yers).

I would not turn tenants away just because they are not heterosexual. I do insist they do not advertise their doings from my building: hookers cannot stand in front of the building in sexy outfits and gays cannot parade around in their drag clothes. They have to live somewhere and usually are discriminated against by landlords. You may even be able to charge them a little more than you charge a straight tenant. One caution: many straight tenants will harass the gay tenants. Watch for this, and, if it occurs, get rid of the gay before trouble develops. If you have seven gays in an eight-family building and the straight gives them a hard time, get rid of the straight.

When, and if, you mix tenants and sex, keep one important thing in mind—money. The money you make will help stimulate the economy of the country. That's the American way. God bless America!

10. Landlord Associations

There is a saying that fits landlord groups: Misery loves company. This sums up my feelings towards most landlord associations. There is only one reason to belong to any group—personal gain. If you can join a landlord group and profit from it, go ahead. It's your valuable time you are using.

How to Profit from a Landlord Group

A few years ago I joined a group of landlords (for personal gain) that had its problems publicized in the local media. I solved the problems and filled my units. The landlords' problem was that tenants were showing up who didn't fit *their* definition of a tenant. The applicants were the wrong color, size, shape, hadn't worked long enough, or had one too many brats. Some didn't have enough cash for the security deposit.

No professional, self-respecting landlord would rent to this assortment of human garbage. I solved their dilemma with one piece of 8½-by-11-inch paper. It was my rental application. I gave all the landlords in this group hundreds of these applications to give to any tenant they found undesirable. I told them to tell the prospective tenant that their unit was taken and give them my

application. That way the tenant thought the landlord was trying to help them and didn't complain to any antidiscriminatory board. On the bottom of each application was the sentence "Bring this in person to Andy Kane" and my address. My office had tenants lined up with fists full of money waiting to fill my vacancies. I had no advertising expense, except my $10 fee to join the association. The landlords were happy to have me remove the misfits from their door step. They had vacancies and loss of income while my units were full!

Dangers of Landlord Associations

One of the prime dangers of these groups, like any other vigilante group, is they will target a department or individual for attack. They will assail the mayor's office for not having the trash picked up on time and the building inspectors for being too hard on them. If you belong to the group and your name is publicized, you can expect retaliation from the departments and groups the association is attacking. You don't need this kind of trouble.

If there is some whiz-bang landlord association in your area which has just gotten taxes reduced 50 percent or utility bills reduced, it may be interesting to attend a meeting or two. You will get to hear a speaker avidly promote his self-interest (he's a new real estate person trying to sell apartment houses, or an insurance salesman). You will get to see what landlords look like and have cold coffee and stale donuts. Sounds like fun.

Anything that is available to a landlord group is also available to you as an individual. Anyone who addresses a landlord group is obviously interested in furthering his own cause and will be glad to answer any questions you have over the phone.

11. Neighborhood Groups

How do these groups fit in with landlord-tenant relations? Let's just look at the make-up of a typical group of do-gooders. The main reason that they have banded together is to exert pressure on some unfortunate in-

dividual whom they want to conform to the standards set by the group.

When the South Avenue Beautification Committee, the Wedgewood Neighborhood Committee, or the Park Avenue Preservation Club meets, their goal is not beautification or preservation. It is to band together and to attack and harass a landlord or homeowner. The homeowner or landlord probably has committed the heinous crime of not cutting his grass this week or having one too many tenants.

These groups are made up of a leader, several lieutenants and a great many followers. The leader will be someone who wants personal gain—a politician looking for votes, a lawyer looking for clients, a new real estate agent looking for buyers and sellers, or a businessman looking for customers. The lieutenants will be factory-types with dead-end jobs where they pack widgets. The workers are probably all tenants. You won't find many landlords belonging to this group of vigilantes. They put their time to more productive use.

These do-gooders are a useless bunch whose main goal is to deprive some landlord or homeowner of his constitutional right. They are useless because, if someone is keeping goats in his yard in a high-class residential neighborhood, there is already a governmental body paid to correct this situation. There are building inspectors and police departments who are supposed to make your neighborhood clean and safe. We do not need the vigilantes. They are a duplication of effort.

I have a saying that I tell to people who belong to vigilante groups: Do-gooders never do good. I have yet to see some actual good done by a group of do-gooders; however, I have seen harm done by them.

For example, I recently saw a neighborhood group prevent a large discount store from using vacant land that was being used to store outdated construction equipment. Their reasoning was it would cause too much traffic. The zoning board knuckled under to the vigilantes. As a result, 200 potential jobs were eliminated from the area. Two million dollars of construction money did not come into the community. The city will not benefit from real estate taxes that the store would have paid. The area will not benefit from sales tax revenue from the sales of this store. The residents of the area have to travel five miles and waste gas and time to purchase the same items this store would have handled. The vigilantes brag today that they were "successful." Were they?

In another example, an elderly widow rented several rooms in her home to defray escalating expenses. Local zoning required that homeowners not rent to more than three people. This homeowner had five tenants in her six bedroom home. The income she received helped maintain her home in superb condition. The neighborhood do-gooders blew her into the zoning board. After several hearings, she was required to vacate two rooms. Within months the property showed signs of deterioration. She could not keep it up as she had. The loss of income made it impossible for her to do anything but pay the utilities, taxes, and mortgage. Paint began to peel. The yard became overgrown. This deterioration affected the property values in the area. Declining property values affected the do-gooders who had been "successful" in enforcing the zoning law. Were they successful?

In a different case, a landlord owned a block with stores on the first floor and about thirty apartments on the second floor. The tenants were the typical "low lifes," but their rents and the rents from the stores kept the property above water. These tenants, many of whom belonged to the Lake Area Beautification Association, enlisted the aid of the other members of this association and harassed the landlord with complaints about minor building code violations. The landlord was forced to vacate the apartments. Without the income generated from the apartments, the landlord was unable to make the mortgage and tax payments. He lost the building. Then ten stores which provided neighborhood service were forced to close. Some had been in that location for twelve years. The tenants then infiltrated better properties in the area. The city lost the tax revenue. The building is a big eyesore with its graffiti and broken windows. The vigilantes kept the landlord from renting these apartments with substandard units, but did they really win?

In a final example, the neighborhood organization in Charlotte, a suburb of Rochester, New York lobbied against expanding the port located in that community. The residents said that increased traffic would create noise and endanger the children. They did not consider the economic benefit of this port (new jobs, increased business for area merchants, and increased revenue to the local government). The neighborhood association was successful in keeping the port from being enlarged.

The city of Oswego, seventy miles east of Charlotte, encouraged the shipping companies to use their port. They received a few million dollars from the federal government for construction and created many new jobs. Did the Charlotte association win or did they lose?

How to Handle the Do-Gooders

I hope you never have to handle an association of do-gooders, but if you do, here are some tips.

First, try to get along with them. Offer them $50 as a donation for their projects. Accidentally make the check out to the president or leader. If he says anything about making it out to the organization, say you didn't know the correct name of the group but you knew his name. Slap him on the back and say "I trust you." Tell him to cash it and give it to the association. When this check comes back from the bank, keep it with your valuable documents. If, at a later date, the do-gooders threaten you, claim you have been blackmailed by them. Threaten to call the media and tell them how the leader said he would keep the neighborhood gang off your back for $50. Now he wants more and you refuse to pay. Show the members a copy of the check to the leader. If they don't back off, call the press.

If the above does not work, threaten them with lawsuits for harassment and loss of income from rents. Sue the leader personally. Sue the organization. Sue all! Once they find out that you are not going to take their

abuse without fighting and that they are going to have to pay a lawyer and take time off from work, they will leave you alone. They are basically gutless and will give up easily. You can intimidate them through our courts. That's the American way. God bless America!

12. Inspectors

When an inspector is assigned a property to inspect and returns with a clean bill of health for the property, his superiors immediately think he did not go to the property or he was paid off. To protect himself, he will write some violation on the report. It's equivalent to a night watchman punching his clock as he does his rounds. It's proof that he was there.

Where do you fit in? Your property is perfect and does not require one repair. This inspector may not be able to find something minor and he may write up something major such as paint the house or put on a new roof. The solution is to give him some minor violation to write up. Take the hinge pins out of the fire door and stand it against the wall, take the screws out of the ceiling light and let it hang by the wires, remove a window and leave it in a closet, or choose another small infraction that can be repaired immediately after the inspector leaves.

Some tips on meeting and cooperating with inspectors are helpful. Be on time. Don't object to their suggestions. Never let them enter the property alone (the tenants may influence them). Inform the tenants that many burglars, rapists, muggers, and sex deviates pose as building inspectors. If they let someone in without your accompanying them, they are endangering their lives. This will usually make tenants afraid of letting an inspector in without your knowledge.

Code Violations

Many times your lovely property will not meet strict new codes—most of which are established to pad some manufacturer's pocket or make some tradesman rich.

Take for example electrical codes which require an outlet every so many feet. Many older buildings do not have adequate outlets. The code was definitely devised by the electrical contractor to create more work for themselves. If you don't want to make them wealthy, try this cheap way out. Determine how many oulets are required for the room. If you need two more, take a saber saw, cut two openings, install two two-by-four-inch boxes in the wall, put in the receptacles and put covers on them. Don't bother to hook them up. They are just dummy outlets but inspectors usually don't test the outlets, so you are safe.

Another trick is the numbers game. Let's say you have a fourplex where all the units are similar. A building inspector finds three in apple pie order; the fourth, Apt. B, needs interior painting and a new vent in the bathroom at the approximate cost of $800. You receive notice to correct these violations within thirty days. You can save this cost and time easily. Just switch the letter *B* on the door to *C*. The *C* then goes on *B*. Call for reinspection. Apartment B will pass with flying colors.

Have you ever had a tenant call the building or health inspector to your property? Did he call and ask the inspector to come to 464 Alexander Street, the address on the property? Try changing the house numbers. If your house is numbered 464 and the next house is numbered 468, change yours to 466. That way, when the report is filed, it will be filed for an address that does not exist in the city and county records.

Insurance company inspectors are a fussy lot. They usually take a photo to show the company that they are doing their job. Many times, when I make application for insurance on a substandard property, I supply the photo so the inspector will not go out and take his own. He can make an easy inspection from his office by looking at the photo and then send it along to the company. Incidently, the photo I supply is not of the property I am insuring, but of the nicest house on the same street. If they ever get wise, tell them you had someone take the photo for you and they must have taken the wrong house.

Smoke Detectors

Nice items but most tenants steal them when they move or take the batteries out of them when they need one for their transistor radio. All this means more maintenance for you. The best place to locate them is on the ceiling. This makes it hard for the inspectors to test them and also hard for the tenant to take the batteries. Many landlords do not even put batteries in them.

13. Training Tenants

It is just as necessary for you to train your tenants as it was for Herb Brooks to train his hockey players to perfection so that they could accomplish their mind-boggling victory in the 1980 Winter Olympics at Lake Placid. An untrained tenant is equivalent to an untrained cat or dog that urinates on your floor. You must train your tenants from the very start.

Begin when they call to see your vacancy. You tell them that they can see it at 5 P.M. They say, "I can't make it then. Can I see it at 7 P.M.? The answer is, "No, if you want to see it, be there at 5 P.M. Goodbye." If you start out by letting the tenants tell you what to do, they will never stop. Show them you are the boss.

Tenants are like children with one exception. Children grow up, tenants never do. A child will see how far he can go without punishment, so will a tenant. Tenants will ask for paint, carpeting, storm windows, an air conditioner, humidifier and other things that were not in the apartment when they rented it. They agreed to rent the apartment "as is" for a certain sum, and they will try to badger you into additional luxuries. Tell them, sure you will paint, and the rent will be $35 more per month. Sure you will put on storm windows, and the rent will be $25 more per month. You will be amazed how fast they will stop asking for additional items.

Phone Calls

When I was working for a large corporation, a fellow employee received at least one call per day from a tenant who would call with serious problems—the light in the hall was burned out, the faucet was dripping. He would jump at each call, run over at lunch time and change the bulb, fix the washer and do other assorted chores. The tenant had trained the landlord in this case.

In fifteen years of working and owning property, I can recall only one case when I was bothered by a call at work. A jet fighter plane crashed in my back yard. The reason my tenants do not call is because I trained them to do the simple things for themselves, without bothering me. I tell them when they move in not to call me, that if there is a problem, write it down and give it to me with the rent. If they call, I tell them "Don't call, write it down and give it to me with the rent."

If a tenant calls at 7 P.M. and leaves a message on my answering machine for me to call Mary Davis at 235-1414 for an important message, I do just that. When I get up during the night at about 3:30 A.M. to go to the bathroom, I call Mary. "Mary, this is Andy. I hope I didn't wake you up, but your message said it was very important and I just got home," I say. Do you think she will call me again? I don't think so. I can really think of no possible reason for a tenant to call me at night. If the electricity goes off, pipes break, or whatever, they can get along until morning.

Impress them with the fact that you are not going to get upset over their minor problems. You are not going to rush over and change a fuse at 10 P.M. They will get the message.

Many people ask if I have an unlisted number. Certainly not. What if someone wants to call me and invite me to a party with all kinds of chicks and booze and my number is unlisted? I would miss a good time and that's why I am a landlord in the first place, to have a good time. My name is not just in the phone book once. It is under every possible classification. It is under realtors, real estate, appraisers, apartments, rentals, rooming houses and in the *A*s as Andy Kane and in the *K*s as Kane, Andy. If a tenant was inclined to call me, he would have no problem finding my number.

If a tenant does call, discourage him from calling again. I answered the phone one day and a tenant excitedly told me that someone had broken into his apartment. I calmly said, "I think you have the wrong number. The number for the police is 911." Do you think that tenant will call back?

Tenants may be trained using the same methods you would use to train any other animal. Reward them for good behavior, punish them for bad behavior. If they are good, reward them by letting them stay. If they are bad, kick them out. Kick them out in the presence of other tenants and you will reinforce the remaining tenants' training.

Lists

Many tenants will make long "grocery" lists of repairs and present them to the landlord. There is a crack in the bathroom window, not enough water pressure, the grass needs cutting, the air conditioner is too noisy, and so on. When the tenant presents you with his list that looks like a six-year-old's Christmas list, don't even look at it. Immediately crush it in your hand and throw it into the tenant's wastebasket. Tell him that when you want a list, you will make it. Since he spent an hour making this list and you threw it away without looking at it, he will probably not waste time doing it again.

It is very important to train tenants so that they do not disturb you. One of the blessings of being a landlord is setting your own hours. Once you let ignorant tenants set your hours, you are finished. You might as well go to work in a factory like 80 percent of the zombies in America. You are a landlord to be your own boss. Don't let anyone take that away.

14. Beauty and Beast

First impressions are always important. I am sure you have heard that beauty is only skin deep. But how many fat, ugly girls get asked for a date? Good-looking ones have them lined up. I am not saying that the fat, ugly woman might not have a heart of gold once you become acquainted, but as long as there are good-looking girls available, why bother? There is just as much chance that the good-looking one has a heart of gold. The point I'm getting at is that for you to have the beasts (tenants) lined up waiting for your beauty (apartment house), she must be appealing.

A little bit of money spent on an entrance will create a desire in the tenant to rent. Many will make up their minds when they get out of the car in front of your property and see the window box with the geraniums, the bright red entrance door with the gold knocker, the red rug running up the stairs and across the porch, the impressive entry with a chandelier, the mirror in a gold frame on the wall and several hanging plants. All this leading them into a cold water flat! They will have their money in their hand before they see the apartment.

I have found this technique quite successful. It

both attracts tenants and pacifies building inspectors and neighborhood groups that prowl areas looking for property to complain about. When they see how nice my property appears from the front, they seldom look farther. Many buildings I own are painted in *front* annually, on the sides when they need it, and in back, *never*. It works wonders.

If you don't believe this works, think about all of the plush looking hotel lobbies you have entered. They look strictly class. You plunk down your money, get your key, walk through the scrumptious lobby, take the gold and glass elevator to the fifth floor and walk into Room 511. The last time it was decorated was for the Elks' Convention in 1956. There is a nice, big cockroach sitting on the dresser watching a soap opera on the black and white TV.

The lobby did it. Let it work for you. Razzle-dazzle them and take their money. That's the American way. God bless America!

15. Filling Vacancies

What do you do when you have a vacancy? Run an ad in the local paper, sit back, and wait for the phone to ring? Great system if the market is depressed in your area and tenants are desperate for housing. But that procedure may not always work. I am going to share some really unique ways of keeping your units on the black side of your ledger. Some cost much less than a classified ad.

Bounty Hunters

Back in the 1800s when a criminal was wanted, the local sheriff put a bounty on his head—$100, dead or alive. Some shifty, unscrupulous, heartless slob who did not care about his fellow man went out, shot the criminal through the back, and dragged him in for the payoff. Do you notice a similarity between the bounty hunter and your existing tenants? Certainly the same characteristics. The bounty system works just as well today, only you should specify that they be brought in alive, if possible. This is how it works.

When you have a vacancy, tell all the tenants that you will give them $5 off next month's rent if they find a tenant for you. They will bust their asses for that bounty. They have an advantage over you in locating

tenants. Remember: Birds of a feather, flock together. They associate with tenants in their employment and recreation. You are not going to run into a potential tenant in your country club atmosphere. But while they are drinking a flat beer in a sleazy pub after work, they will probably be with many potential tenants for your unit. Have your tenant bring them over. They will probably talk the tenant into renting from you. If they don't, they don't get their bounty.

Classified Advertising

One of the most expensive methods of filling a vacancy is classified ads. Depending on where you live and the size of your paper, the rates may be a few cents to several dollars per line. This can mount up rapidly. Some papers offer a discount, if you sign a contract for daily advertising. You should carefully evaluate this contract method to determine if it is economical for you. Do you have enough vacancies to make it practical? Do you want calls every day or just on certain days?

Since classified is expensive, you should do all you can to assure maximum results. Many years ago I noticed a phenomenon. I had two similar apartments for rent. One was about $25 more than the other. The more expensive one was getting about thirty calls a day and the other, in a better area and cheaper, was getting only one or two. I set out to discover why. The expensive one was on Aab Street and the cheaper one on West Avenue. I discovered that prospective tenants opened to the classification they were interested in (furnished, unfurnished, city, or country), began calling the first ad, and worked down until they found a place that suited their humble needs. Since the classifieds were in alphabetical order, a vacancy that was in the As received the maximum number of inquiries and the one in the Zs received few or no inquiries. The ideal arrangement would be to buy property only on streets that begin with A, although that's not too practical or logical. The next best thing is to have your vacancies listed under the A no matter where they are located. When you have your next vacancy on Merriman Street take a city map and look for a major street near Merriman which begins with an A.

Start your ad: "Acorn Street area, six-room . . ." When the potential tenant calls about the apartment on Acorn Street you tell him it is two blocks west of Acorn on Merriman, near Cross Street. You will be amazed at the number of calls you get by using the alphabet to your advantage.

Hint

If you are ever looking for a used car, lawn mower, furniture, or any other item in the classifieds, start at the bottom and work up. You will get the best deals because your call may be the only one the seller received. If he is anxious, you can name your own price.

Wording Your Ad

Your time is worth bucks, so you only want the calls that are from serious renters. If you have an apartment that you don't want kids in, say so. If you will take kids or welfare, say so. If it has a feature that is desirable such as gas heat, heat paid, pool, parking, or cable TV, indicate it. It may cost a buck more but it will save you time in rejecting calls for features that are not available and from unqualified tenants.

For example:

"Ambrose, 6-room, upper, parking, pool, cable, kids, pets welcome, no welfare, $350 includes utilities, security. 482-3274."

An ad like this will only attract a tenant with a need for this type of accommodation. By including the price, you ferret out the rascals who cannot afford the apartment. Your calls will be more productive and your time will not be wasted.

Save More Time

We now have the ad placed to attract the most attention and written to attract exactly the tenant you want, so why talk to these simple-minded jerks at all?

Since all the information is in the ad, the only reason to talk to these creatures is to tell them to be at 655 Ambrose at 5 P.M. There are two ways you can avoid spending your time talking to them. Add the address to the ad (Ambrose, 655) and in place of the phone number, insert "Shown at 5 P.M. daily." Now you just show up at 5 P.M. Don't let the tenants talk you into going at their convenience. Tell them the *only* time you are showing this apartment is at 5 P.M. If they want to see it, they should be there. If you go at their time, they have dictated conditions to you and will never stop.

If you do not want to put the extra information in the ad, buy a telephone answering device for your phone. Leave a message saying, "The apartment at 655 Ambrose Street is still available. I will be showing it at 5 P.M. today and tomorrow (for those who call after 5 P.M.). Ambrose is off Lake Avenue, near the First Methodist Church. Please be on time because I have another appointment at 5:30 P.M. in another part of town."

Save Even More Time

Don't go at all. If there is another tenant in the building, have them show it for you. When a tenant expresses interest, have that one tenant contact you with the money. This way you only deal with one jerk, not a gang of them.

I suggest showing the apartment at only one specific time. I know of many landlords who stagger appointments to show the apartment, so that the tenants are not there all at once. He may be there for two hours. Two or three no-shows leave him in an empty apartment for an hour. By having twelve prospective tenants come at the same time, you create the fear that someone else is going to rent it, if they don't act right away. Something like panic buying takes place. Each one wants to beat out the other. I have even heard prospective tenants fight over who was going to get it. If only one person at a time is looking at an apartment, the competitive spirit is not present.

Signs

For Rent signs are excellent and when compared to bounties or classifieds, they have several advantages. You pay for the sign only once where you pay a bounty each time a vacancy occurs and pay for an ad each time an apartment is vacant. Statistics show that the most likely person to rent your apartment is someone who has a tie to the neighborhood, someone who works in the area, has family or friends in the area or presently lives in the area. A sign will be seen by all of these.

The sign should contain all the necessary information. Don't go to the hardware store and buy an iridescent eight-by-ten-inch plastic For Rent sign. They are worthless since they don't tell anything about what is for rent. I can see only one place that these signs could be of any value. That is on a hooker's back. Then there is no need for additional information, except price and, of course, that would be negotiable anyway.

Have a sign painter make a sign big enough to be seen from the street. Include pertinent information, such as For Rent, Furnished 6-Room Apt., $350, incl. utilities. 482-3200. Carry these signs in your trunk. As soon as you are notified of a pending vacancy, put the sign up. You may very well rent the apartment immediately and not have a vacancy, the cost of an ad, or bounty. Give it a try.

Rent Referral Agencies

These are agents who compile a list of various apartments and their features. For a fee from a prospective tenant, they make the information available to them. Nearly every big city has one or many. Some are good, some are not. You are not charged for their service. Their revenue is from the prospective tenants. I would advise using their services whenever possible. It can't hurt you. I own one of the largest rent referral agencies in Rochester, New York and we have referred hundreds of tenants to landlords who would not have gotten them otherwise.

What Method Is Best for Filling Vacancies

If you are a hunter, the solution is obvious. A shotgun blast will bring down more birds than a bullet. Use the shotgun approach. Use ads, bounty, signs, and referral agents. You cannot afford to have a vacant unit. It is money out of your pocket. Get all the money you can. Money brings happiness and I want you to be happy. It's the American way. God bless America.

16. Subleasing

One of the best ways to lose control of your building is to allow the tenants any choice in who is to occupy the property. Allowing the tenants to sublet the remaining portion of their lease is crazy. Many landlords allow a sublet clause in their leases with the condition that they have the final approval. You are looking for trouble if this clause is in any lease you use. Here are some examples of subleasing.

The tenant and you are not seeing eye to eye and he decides to move and sublet his apartment. He places an ad at his expense and interviews several potential tenants. He finds the ideal one to occupy your unit, a filthy, fat, unshaven bum who works as a garbage collector and usually brings home some items he gets attached to during the day like an old tire or couch. Obviously you don't want him but try to refuse him. He has picked up garbage for thirteen years and has excellent credit. Three other guys on the garbage truck give him excellent credit references. His employer says he has never missed a day's work. You are going to be in court if you refuse to rent to him. Your present tenant has you where he wants you.

The problem could have been avoided if your

lease contained a clause which does not allow the tenant to sublet but instead allows you to seek a new tenant. Your expenses for subleasing are deductable from the present tenant's security deposit. This way you are in control.

Another interesting example of a sublease came to my attention lately. A tenant moved into an apartment and later in the same month, told the landlord he had been transferred. His rent was $400 per month and his security deposit was also $400. He said he would advertise and sublease the apartment. The landlord was happy that the tenant was going to do all the work for him. His happiness was short-lived.

The tenant prepared a nice-looking sublease agreement assigning the lease that he had signed. The new tenant was to pay $400 rent for the following month and pay the $400 security to the existing tenant. The existing tenant took this sublease out and made ten copies. He also made ten shiny, new keys. He placed an ad in the paper and rented the apartment to the first ten people who came to inspect it. He gave them all a key and said he would be out by 10 A.M. on the first of the following month. He collected $8,000 from these potential tenants. Can you imagine the confusion, fighting and near-riot when, at 10 A.M. on the first, ten moving vans arrived and ten tenants had shiny new keys, all for the same apartment? The landlord is still trying to straighten out the mess. Again, it could have been avoided by not allowing subleasing.

Keep the story of the ten keys in mind. If you ever have a string of bad luck in Las Vegas, find a landlord who was not smart enough to buy this book, lease an apartment, make ten shiny new keys and so on.

17. Actor Tenants

The title immediately brings to mind, depending on your vintage, actors from Charlie Chaplin and Errol Flynn to John Wayne or John Travolta. All of the above were paid fantastic amounts of money for acting. Some received millions for just one movie. Do you know any-

one greater than these movie greats? Someone who earned more for their acting? I bet you do.

Do you remember when you went to collect your $300 rent last month and the wily tenant in Apt. 6A told you he didn't have the rent " 'Cause ma muther took sick in Louisiana and I sent it to her." That ridiculous excuse takes five seconds to say. He cheated you out of $300 in just five seconds.

My theory is that when you do not get $300 from your tenant, you have lost really $600, since you must add $300 of your money to make up for the $300 loss. The tenant, for his Academy Award act, has bilked you out of $600 for five seconds' work, $7,200 per minute, or $432,000 per hour. Not bad salary for an aspiring actor. And he's not even paying his union dues or income tax.

How to Bring the Curtain Down

As you may have noticed in other chapters, I believe in an eye for an eye, tooth for a tooth, and fighting fire with fire. You must become a *better* actor than your resident actor. Acting school is now in session.

I have never heard a really believable excuse so I have counterattacked with excuses which match the caliber of their excuses. Some examples are below.

Excuse: I had a tenant return from Puerto Rico and tell me that he did not have my rent money, because he had to make an emergency trip to see his critically-ill mother.

Reply: "You mean you're a doctor. I never knew that." (Reasoning: The sick person needs only a doctor or medical attention, not visits from relatives.)

Excuse: "It was Christmas."

Reply: "Christmas has been on the calendar for twelve months. It was not unexpected." (Same holds true for Easter, first day of school, and kid's school clothes.)

Excuse: "My check didn't come." (Or it was lost in the mail.)

Reply: "You're a liar. Have welfare (or work or whatever) call me before 5 P.M. today or move out."

Allowing that the mail is run by the most incompetent people on earth, have you ever had a letter or a check lost? I have not and you probably have not either. I send thousands of checks, letters, and documents through the mail and have never had one lost.

Excuse: "I was mugged." (Their money taken.)
Reply: "Go mug somebody else." (Get it back.)

Conclusion

You should *never* believe tenants' excuses. If you once believe their excuses, you will be set up for dozens of encores. If you want to see action, go to the theater. It's much cheaper. When the tenant resorts to excuses and acting, he's on his last legs. Give him a deadline to get the rent on the *same* day. Don't give him a week or two days. Give him a short deadline and, if he doesn't have the rent, kick him out.

You are running a business, not a charity. You pay taxes so the government can house the deadbeats in low-income projects. Let the government do its job. That's the American way. God bless America!

18. Captive Tenants

Do you ever wish that your tenants were permanent with no possibility for a vacancy? It is possible to obtain permanent tenants.

If you have single-family dwellings with four or five bedrooms, or large apartments, you can nearly achieve the goal of never having to worry about the tenant moving. Just rent to a tenant with a lot of screaming, filthy kids. Ten or twelve are excellent. They can't move out. No landlord would take them.

I use this technique when a property is getting near the end of the line. I have one particular property that has paid for itself about eight times. It is in need of paint and other cosmetic work, but reasonably sound. I found a nice family with twelve kids. Two of the older ones were pregnant, so the grand total would shortly be sixteen. I arranged for them to occupy the property on a lease which calls for them to make any repairs and keep the property up for the privilege of occupying the property and paying rent. This property has now paid me another $6,000 without my investing one additional cent. Before hitting on the large-family solution, I had considered abandoning the property instead of renovating it to the degree that would attract an average tenant. This way has worked out extremely well. The tenant is happy and I am very, very happy.

If you have property in an area that is going downhill, you may want to consider a rooming house for undesirables. Let's take a large single-family dwelling in a rundown area that would normally rent for $250 per month. It has four bedrooms, living room, kitchen, dining room and bath. You convert the living room and dining room into bedrooms and you have a total of six sleeping rooms and the tenants share the kitchen and bath. These rooms rent for $100 each (or $25 per week) for an income of $600 per month compared to $250 per month. The tenants stay for long periods of time because, due to their characters (winos and junkies), no other landlord wants them. Captive tenants! An ideal situation.

Many cities have ordinances against this type of conversion. Check with city zoning people as to how many nonrelated people you can have in one single-family dwelling. I once had a friend who was a retired attorney and had an illegal rooming house that the city was cracking down on. He beat them by adopting all eleven bums. This then made them all brothers. The ordinance stated specifically that no more than three unrelated people could live in the same house and since these eleven bums were all "brothers," nothing could be done to stop it.

Over the years, I have converted many single-family dwellings into rooming houses without it being legal. The profit you can squeeze out of this type of house, until you are caught, is enormous. I used the surplus revenue generated by converting a single into a rooming house to buy a new Cadillac Eldorado annually. The difference in rent between a single and a rooming house was about $4,000 a year, just enough with my old Caddie each year to trade. All the tenants were on welfare so this was truly a "welfare Cadillac."

One word of caution. When you crowd this many bums and winos into one area, you are coming close to what caused the riots at Attica prison a few years back. I had killings in my rooming houses and I believe it was a direct result of so many undesirables in one area.

You should spend as little time as possible at the property to avoid being involved in any violence. Collect rent in the daylight hours only. Avoid Friday and Saturday when they are usually high or drunk and always carry your gun.

Captive tenants provide a good steady income, but they may turn on you in a moment. Keep your guard up and keep collecting the extra bucks from these misfits. You are actually doing the country a service by housing these bums. You should get a medal, you good American, you. God bless America.

19. Voice Pagers

Landlords have many devices to make their days easier. There are telephone answering machines, mobile phones for the car, pocket calculators for prorating rents and, most importantly, pagers. The pager can be rented or purchased. Anyone can call you and leave a ten second message which you receive instantly.

If you use a maintenance man to service various apartments, you can better utilize his time by being in direct contact with him no matter where he is. If he is on the roof of the building two miles away, you can get a message to him instantly. If you have a pager and a tenant calls the office with the message that you are to pick up the rent and you are just leaving the parking lot of the same property, your office can call you and you will save time and gas. Your wife can call you and remind you to bring home a quart of milk. But let me mention how pagers can be used in unique ways to make more money and your life easier.

The Brush Off

How often have you been in the predicament of trying to get rid of some tenant whom you didn't want to rent to? Many times, when you try to brush off one of these crummy jerks, they take you before some housing or racial council. This can all be avoided with planned use of the pager.

Let's take this example: You have many calls on a vacant apartment. You tell them all to meet you there at 2 P.M. Have your secretary, wife, or friend call you on the pager at 2:10 P.M. She is instructed to say, "The people who looked at the apartment this morning just came into the office and rented it." Obviously the tenants who are looking at the apartment will hear this. If they are undesirables, just shrug your shoulders and say "Sorry folks." They will hit the road thinking that you are a nice guy. If, when the message comes over the pager, you want to rent to the tenants who are looking at the apartment, simply say "Don't worry folks. She's not talking about this apartment." Then take their money. You deserve it. That's the American way. God bless America.

20. Energy

When I first began owning and renting investment property in 1959, heating oil was selling for about 15¢ per gallon. The oil company would also give me a discount if I consumed a large amount of fuel oil. During the 1979-80 heating season, the cost of fuel oil in the northeast was in excess of $1.20 per gallon. In the days of cheap energy, you would have been foolish to waste money on insulation or storm windows. Now, with our present energy crisis and the still-rising cost of all types of energy, you would be foolish not to take measures to reduce energy consumption.

Any expenditure to reduce costs and conserve energy should be carefully evaluated to insure that you are not wasting your hard-earned bucks. What payback will you receive from your investment for a new furnace, insulation, or other energy-saving improvement? Will it pay for itself over a period of five, ten, or fifteen years? Will it add to the resale value of the property? Are you going to own the property long enough to recover the cost through savings? All are important factors. Don't be badgered into investing in energy-saving features by pressure from governmental groups, neighborhood groups, or home improvement salesmen. It's your money. Be sure the return is there before you sign on the dotted line.

One important factor in any decision you make should be whose money will be saved. If you are paying heat, it's your money being saved. If the tenant is paying for the heat, your investment will save them money. What advantage is there in saving money for the tenant? None to you that I know of. If you insulate the tenants' building and they save $10 a month on heat, they will just squander the money on something stupid anyway. You could raise their rent $10 and justify your cost that way.

I would say that the following investments should return their cost to you in the specified time to make them practical:

Item	Return Time
Insulation	5 years
*New Furnace	7 years
Storm Windows, Doors	2 years
*Water Heater	2 years
Flue Damper	3 years
Timers and Computer Controls for Heat & Air	5 years

*I would never replace a good furnace or water heater just to save energy, but when you replace these items, you should insist on energy-saving features, such as electric pilots and flue dampers.

The Tenant and Energy

The tenant *may* conserve energy if he is paying for it. I say may because I have seen tenants leave lights on when not in use, leave doors and windows open when the heat is on, and hundreds of other wasteful things. The odds are that a tenant will be *more inclined* to save energy if he is paying. It is a certainty that he will not do one thing to save energy if the landlord is footing the bill. If you are paying for utilities, there are steps you may take to save you thousands of dollars in energy costs each year.

Heat

This is one major area where you can cut costs. Analyze your building. Are the tenants all working and out of the property between 8 A.M. and 5 P.M. every day? Eliminate or reduce heat during this period by installing a clock-type timer to shut off the power to the furnace at intervals during the day.

The building is warm at 7 A.M. and will take awhile to cool down. Set the timer to kill the power from 7 A.M. to 10 A.M., turn on for an hour between 10 A.M. and 11 A.M., off 11 A.M. to 3 P.M., and on 3 P.M. to 11 P.M. Most tenants will go to bed by then so they will be comfortable.

Have the furnace turn on again at 1 A.M. for an hour and on at about 4 A.M. to 6 A.M. If you eliminate heat for 25 percent of the day and your heating bill is $10,000 a year, you will save $2,500. That's a good chunk of cash to plow back into buying more apartments or taking a vacation.

You may have to play with the timing to achieve maximum results, but it's worth your time to do it. Each heating system responds differently. A hot water or steam system will have to build up pressure or heat water to respond. Forced air, electric resistance, or heat pump response will be very rapid. Heating systems should be maintained at their maximum efficiency. Just as a car in need of a tune-up will require more fuel to run, so will your heating system if it is not tuned up. Have it serviced regularly.

Forced Air Systems

Check for balance in the system. Each unit should receive the same amount of heat. If one unit is forty feet from the furnace, the damper on that heat run may have to be wide open. An apartment close to the furnace may need to have the damper open only half way. Cold air intakes and returns should be clear of furniture and rugs. It is important to return this used air to the unit for peak efficiency. In this same system, you will find a furnace filter. The purpose of this filter is to eliminate dust from this air system. It will also restrict the flow of air as it becomes clogged. Remove it now and throw it away. The furnace will function much better without it. A little more dust will be on the tenants' filthy furniture but that will be the only noticeable effect.

Hot Water Steam Systems

When radiators are involved, there is always the chance that air will enter the system and fill the upper portion of the radiators. This prevents the hot water or steam from filling the entire radiator and causes inefficient heating. Bleed the radiators until they are full of water or steam. This is done manually or with automatic bleed valves.

Solar

These systems are very good for small units and depend on a certain amount of available sunlight. They are efficient when used correctly and should be checked by a trained technician frequently.

Heat Pumps

Excellent use of available outside warm air. Each year the units become more reliable and should be considered if you are renovating or replacing existing systems.

Humidifier

A must with most systems. Damp air is capable of carrying more heat through the room than dry air.

Thermostat

This is the most important part of any system because it controls the temperature. You should provide only what heat the law requires. Many areas require a 68 degree Fahrenheit setting. That's plenty warm enough. If the tenants are cold, let them wear coats. During the energy crisis of 1979, President Carter requested that thermostats be set at 65 degrees Fahrenheit. I immediately complied with Uncle Sam's desires. When my tenants complained, I called them unpatriotic slobs. They shut right up and I saved a buck or two.

You must be in sole control of the thermostat. This is important. If that thermostat is in a hall, tenants will turn it up. If you put a lock on it, they will put a bag of ice on it. The best way to solve the tampering problem is to have two thermostats, one the tenants can play with and another that controls the heat and is in the basement or hidden in a locked closet. Never let on that there are two thermostats or the sneaky tenants will look for it. Always check the dummy thermostat closely and turn it down a degree or two while the tenants are looking. They will turn it back up as soon as you leave and be pacified. They will actually feel warmer! You have heard of experiments in which two patients are given identical pills but one is a sugar pill and one is medication. Both patients feel better. The thermostat ploy works exactly the same.

Electric

Save money by attending to the obvious, electricity-saving techniques first—using low-wattage bulbs, reducing outdoor lighting, and banning the use of electric Christmas decorations or trees that require lighting.

Then look for the not-so-obvious—timer switches on hall, garage and basement lights. They turn off automatically at a predetermined time.

Water

When replacing faucets, use only the types that require no maintenance of washers. They cost slightly more but eliminate leaky faucets and maintenance time. Eliminate outside hose connections. Let the tenant wash his Edsel at a car wash. One of my locations had an enormous water bill and I could find no leaks. Many inspections revealed everything in apple-pie order. One Sunday I passed by and found ten armored trucks from a local bank parked in front of the property. There was my tenant washing armored trucks. He had a contract to wash twenty trucks every Sunday, using my water! I promptly removed the outside faucet from this place and from all others I own.

Stealing Power or Water

Every meter can be altered. Water meters will usually run backwards if you turn them around. Electric meters can be jumpered, gas meters can be by-passed. All of these practices are done. All I can say is that you could be in trouble if you are caught and you can be killed if you do it wrong.

Tenant's Appliances

Stoves, refrigerators, washers, and dryers all consume energy. The tenant being shiftless and lazy will

probably not keep his appliances in good, efficient, working order. If they are not defrosted or maintained, complain until they are fixed.

Conclusion

One of the most abused items in any apartment building is the utilities. If you lose control of these, due to tenant misuse, your profit will suffer drastically. Don't let these sneaky creatures, called tenants, rob you of your profits.

Be a good American, conserve energy (and save money). That's the American way. God bless America!